Norway Travel Guide

The Most Up-to Date Pocket Guide to Discover Norway's Hidden Treasure | Travel Making the Most of Your Time and Plan the Nicest Trip to Land of midnight Sun

Fabian Burns

© Copyright 2023 - All rights reserved.

The content contained within this book may not be reproduced, duplicated, or transmitted without direct written permission from the author or the publisher.

Under no circumstances will any blame or legal responsibility be held against the publisher, or author, for any damages, reparation, or monetary loss due to the information contained within this book. Either directly or indirectly.

Legal Notice:

This book is copyright protected. This book is only for personal use. You cannot amend, distribute, sell, use, quote, or paraphrase any part, or the content within this book, without the author's or publisher's consent.

Disclaimer Notice:

Please note the information contained within this document is for educational and entertainment purposes only. All effort has been executed to present accurate, up-to-date, and reliable, complete information. No warranties of any kind are declared or implied. Readers acknowledge that the author does not render legal, financial, medical, or professional advice. The content within this book has been derived from various sources. Please consult a licensed professional before attempting any techniques outlined in this book.

By reading this document, the reader agrees that under no circumstances is the author responsible for any direct or indirect losses incurred due to the use of the information contained within this document, including, but not limited to, errors, omissions, or inaccuracies.

Table of Contents

Introduction 7

Chapter 1: Getting Ready For Your Trip 9

    Learning some practical Norwegian idioms and terminology with a native 10

    Weather in Norway 13

    best fashion advice from Norway 14

    Be prepared for the weather 15

    Things to avoid in Norway 16

    Do not anticipate the alcohol to be very potent 17

    Don't offend the King in public 17

    Look up the cost of taxis 18

    Spend time in nature 22

Chapter 2: Facts About Norway 24

Chapter 3: Key Places To Visit In Norway 31

Chapter 4: Tourists Attraction Sites 39

    1. Oslo 39

2. Bergen..........44

3. Tromso..........46

4. Trondheim..........48

5. Lofoten..........51

6. Stavanger..........53

7. Alesund..........55

Trail for Hiking to Preikestolen..........58

National Park of Jotunheimen..........60

Maihaugen Open-Air Museum..........62

Kristiansand Zoo..........64

Svalbard Museum..........67

Norwegian Aviation Museum..........69

Chapter 5: Famous Architectural Wonders in Norway. 71

The National Museum Architecture, Oslo..........71

Utsikten Viewpoint, Gaularfjellet..........72

Eggum, Lofoten..........72

Tverrfjellhytta, Dovre..........74

Trollveggen Visitor Center, More OgRomesdal 75

Hauklandstranda, Lofoten..78

Chapter 6: Best restaurants in Norway 80

Maaemo. 81

Mathus Peder Hiort 82

Aunegarden 84

Chapter 7: The Best Accommodation In Norway 86

Chapter 8: Best Souvenirs to buy in Norway. 93

Sweets from Norway..94

Vikings...95

Lucky Trolls 95

The Decorations in Pewter...96

Conclusion 98

Introduction

Every country in the world has its own recognizable features, characteristics, culture and customs. Norway has always been one of the most fascinating and outstanding tourist destinations in the world, known for its exceptional beauty and diversity. To say that Norway has something for everyone is an understatement. Nestled firmly in the heart of Northern Europe, my country will leave you speechless with its rugged coastline, majestic fjords and beautiful islands. The richness of Norway is indisputable.

The natural landscape is breathtaking and dramatic, while the country's mountainous terrain crisscrossed with islands and dotted with fjords mark most of the territory. Norway, or officially the Kingdom of Norway is bordered by Sweden, Finland, and Russia to the east. Exploring Norway can take days, weeks or months or as long as you want.

It is a thoroughly modern sovereign and unitary monarchy with beautiful villages, towns, and cities. It is also a relatively small country, with a population of approximately 5,100,000 people. Famous for its extensive coastline, charming trolls, and rich history, Norway is a place like no other. I believe that it is the combination of these impressive geographical features, unspoiled nature, windswept vistas and unique coastal life that creates a truly quintessentially tourist experience. Numerous cities of interest include Oslo, the capital of Norway; Bergen, the second largest city in Norway, steeped in history and famed for many legendary attractions; Trondheim with its stunning architecture; Tromsø, the best gateway to the Arctic with an abundance of things to do.

Chapter 1:
Getting Ready For Your Trip

You can get practical planning advice from this chapter for your trip to Norway. Going somewhere new can be stressful, especially if you have a lot of things to think about. Whether you are a seasoned traveler or you are making last-minute travel plans, there are a few things you should never forget, especially if you want to get the most out of your time in my nation. Norway is generally a highly safe place to travel to because of its low level of crime.

However, keep in mind to exercise caution at night, particularly in Norway's bigger cities. It's also a good idea to take good care of your personal property. You only need to be cautious about pickpockets while using ATMs to obtain cash; you don't need to carry much cash. Unfortunately, there are more and more thefts and pickpockets. Call 112 in case of emergency. The number to call for all emergency services in our country is this. Ask for assistance from the locals if you feel unsafe, and carry your phone at all times.

You should also be aware of Norway's diverse wildlife, which differs from that in various other European nations. For instance, Svalbard is home to a variety of marine mammals, including the Arctic fox, polar bears, and others. For inexperienced travelers, polar bears in particular, can pose a serious threat. It's also crucial to remember that Norway only has one kind of dangerous snake. The European adder can be found all around the nation, but fortunately, most bites are not fatal.

Numerous bothersome insects, such as ticks, are also frequently observed during the summer. Through a bite, they can spread viral encephalitis and Lyme's disease. Furthermore, they actually can ruin your enjoyment of the summer. You should exercise some common sense safeguards even if these instances are uncommon. Always choose for long pants over shorts, especially if you intend to travel to some remote locations. You should see a doctor as soon as you can since these insects can bite you in very harmful ways.

Learning some practical Norwegian idioms and terminology with a native

There are several different languages spoken in the nation, including Norwegian, Danish, and Swedish. These two languages have a lot in common. However, most people in Norway speak English as well. It is a good idea to learn some fundamental Norwegian words and phrases before traveling, and you'll discover that conversing in a new tongue can be both entertaining and thrilling. I assure you that it's simpler than it seems. So here are some foundational terms in Norwegian.

Yes = Ja

No = Nei

Thank you = Takk

Please = Vær så snill

Excuse me = Unnskyld meg

Hello = Hallo

Goodbye = Ha det

I do not understand = Jeg forstår ikke

Where is ...? = Hvor er ...?

Train = Tog

Bus = Buss

Tram = Trikk

I would like to buy... = Jeg vil gjerne kjøpe...

Police station = Politistasjon
Hospital = Sykehus

Good morning = God morgen

Good night = God natt

How are you? = Hvordan går det?

Help! = Hjelp!

One = En
Two = To
Three = Tre
Four = Fire
Five = Fem
Six = Seks
Seven = Syv
Eight = Åtte
Nine = Ni
Ten = Ti

Day = Dag
Week = Uke
Month = Måned
Year = År
Today = I dag
Yesterday = I går
Tomorrow = I morgen

This list of useful Norwegian phrases will help you in case of an emergency.

Weather in Norway

Many people believe that Norway experiences year-round cold and precipitation, yet the length of the winter fluctuates. Norway generally has chilly but temperate weather, largely because to the Gulf Stream. However, if you venture outside, you should always be ready for a change in the weather.

In general, prices tend to increase dramatically during the Northern Lights, and June and July are the busiest months in the nation. The typical temperature range throughout the winter is between 1°C and 2°C. Of course, snowfall differs from place to place. Be ready for a lot of snow if northern Norway is on your schedule. It fortunately doesn't stay on the ground for very long. Some locations have permanent glaciers even in the summer, and the winters are frequently exceedingly dark. Norway is a country with four distinct seasons, although the winter and spring are when it is most picturesque.

Visitors have an excellent opportunity to visit Norway in the spring. The month of May in particular is ideal for family vacations to Norway. Although it is often the finest time of year to travel, several of Norway's top tourist destinations can get quite busy. In many parts of Norway, you can typically expect moderate weather from May through August. The days are often long, sunny, and pleasant during the summer.

The summers can get a little heated. Summer is a terrific season to explore Norway's coast and lakes by kayaking, canoeing, sailing, and fishing. One of the greatest times to travel to Norway is in the fall. It's the best season to travel because the days are so lovely and there are fewer people around, allowing you to see the country at your own speed. You should be aware that Norway has significant seasonal variations in its daylight hours. Be ready because the weather in Norway can change rapidly, just like it does across all of Scandinavia.

best fashion advice from Norway

Norwegians typically wear well-groomed, casual clothing, and outside of the cities, sports and outdoor gear are common.

It's a good idea to bring long pants, long sleeve shirts, and boots in any season. Add extra layers of warmth for the winter, such as sweaters, fleece, and knitwear.

You'll be glad you packed some long thermal underwear for extra warmth.

Since light wool regulates body temperature naturally, it is a great material to wear next to skin. It keeps you dry when it's humid, wicks moisture away when it's hot, and doesn't retain odors even after prolonged usage.

Even in chilly temperatures, the sun can still be very intense, so pack sunscreen (we recommend the Riemann P20 range for 10-hour protection).

Wear sunglasses as well because the sun's rays will reflect off the water in lakes and fjords as well as the immaculate surface of the snow.

You may also want to pack something to protect your cheeks and lips from the frigid, dry air. For children's faces, protective clothing like balaclava caps and large amounts of lip balm are highly advised.

If it's going to snow when you go, bring snow goggles; they'll be quite useful.

When trekking, put on solid shoes, and never leave the house without a snack, a drink, warm clothing, etc. Remember to bring your camera, too!

Given how much Norwegians love wearing wool clothing, knitwear will blend in well.

Be prepared for the weather.

During the summer, bring a choice of clothing for warm and cold, rainy and dry weather (June, July, and August).

Sunny summer days can be warm enough to wear shorts and t-shirts if you're not too far north. However, it's advisable to always have a sweater and raincoat on hand, especially if you intend to embark on longer excursions or hikes, as the weather could suddenly change.

In April and August, when mosquitoes are most active, be careful to pack insect/mosquito repellant.

For the frigid months of November through March, you should also bring a heavy coat, gloves, a warm cap, scarf, and especially robust boots with soft rubber soles.

Because even medium soles become incredibly hard in the bitter cold, you should get shoes with soft rubber soles. In order to avoid snow from getting caught between the tracks and making them dangerously slick, make sure there are plenty of gaps between them as well.

Bring a lightweight raincoat or waterproof jacket with you everywhere you go because it rains all year long.

Things to avoid in Norway

Norway is a very welcoming nation. The moment you set foot in the country; the people will extend a warm welcome to you. As we've already mentioned, Norway is a convenient country, and you can always wander around without feeling threatened. The government is concerned about the welfare of the visitors, and the citizens of Norway collaborate with the visitors to make the nation a joyful and liberated place. Although the likelihood of encountering an uncomfortable circumstance is quite low in Norway, things might occasionally go wrong and you may find yourself in an awkward situation. But don't worry; we've given you a comprehensive list of the country's dos and don'ts. Just heed the guidelines, and you may travel across Norway without encountering any problems.

Do not anticipate the alcohol to be very potent.

In Norway, Vinmonopolet is the exclusive distributor of alcoholic beverages. Since the 1920s, Norway has had a history of alcoholism, and the government has done an excellent job of stopping or reducing it there. The nation is not, however, a dry one; you can purchase alcohol there. Vinonopolets sells alcohol in Norway, as well as any spirit with an alcohol content of greater than 4.7 percent. Once you enter a vinmonopolet outlet, you have a wide range of options. The vinmonopolets are present in almost all of Norway's major cities, so you won't encounter any difficult circumstances when trying to purchase alcohol. Just make sure you go to the proper location. Look into the store hours because they are not always open. The majority of the time, the alcohol stores in Norway are open from 10 a.m. to 5 p.m. on Mondays, Tuesdays, and Wednesdays, from 10 a.m. to 6 p.m. on Thursdays and Fridays, from 10 a.m. to 3 p.m. on Saturdays, and they are probably closed on Sundays, so be cautious. However, you can always find them at the stores if you have a beer hankering. You must purchase them before 8 o'clock because supermarkets in Norway are permitted to sell alcohol before then.

Don't offend the King in public.

Norway is one of the very few nations that still has its own king, giving it an incredibly old aesthetic. A significant number of decisions, or, to be more precise, administrative decisions in Norway, are made by the royal family because the monarch of Norway holds a very prominent position in

Norwegian administration. Norway's citizens are hence quite concerned about its constitutional monarchy. By disregarding their constitutional monarchy, you run the risk of getting yourself into awkward positions. The nation of Norway holds the current king, King Harald V, in the highest regard. Nearly all of Norway's former monarchs, as well as the royal family and the current king, have an important role to play in the country's governance of its citizens. The people of the nation adore them because of their prominent status. Even though King Harald V is currently 80 years old, he still manages to have a great sense of humor and deliver stirring addresses to his nation's citizens. You can get yourself into trouble if you publicly criticize the ruler of the nation.

Look up the cost of taxis.

In Norway, taxis are not a very common mode of local transportation, and few people use them to get around the cities. In other situations, we would advise against using taxis; yet, if you find yourself in an emergency scenario, there is nothing you can do except use cabs. Although the taxis in Norway are quite safe and helpful to the customers, the high cost of the rates, along with the high cost of the road, prevents them from being very well-liked in the nation. The typical fares for taxis when traveling inside cities range from $60 to $150. If you are planning a low-cost trip to Norway, we are confident that you would not want to spend that much money. Other forms of transportation in Norway are quite practical, readily available, and will carry you anywhere you need to go. You will enjoy the finest of

Norway if you keep an eye out for the numerous transportation options available there and do some study.

Watch your drinking duration.

As we have already indicated, Norway faces a number of alcohol-related problems. If you intend to drink, bear in mind a variety of implications and details. Although not frequently or heavily, Norwegians do drink. The government has made good efforts to reduce alcohol usage nationwide. Since 1920, when the state began taking action on this matter, not all stores in Norway have been allowed to serve alcohol to tourists. The amount of what you drink is now in question. When visiting Norway, you must choose your drinks carefully. The best time to go out and celebrate in the country is on Friday night and into the early evening. But on days other than Friday, we advise you to have a glass of wine while dining out. Although Norwegians are not particularly conservative, they may discourage you from drinking in public on weekdays because of administrative restrictions.

Get the umbrella.

If you are vacationing in Norway, we advise obtaining a raincoat rather than an umbrella. The raincoat will be useful because Norway's weather is so erratic. If you have an umbrella, there won't be any serious issues, however you could have some trouble adjusting to the weather. As we have already indicated, the weather in Norway is very erratic, and it may rain briefly fifteen times every day. If you are traveling to the stunning land of Norway, we are sure you would like to bring a camera with you. However, an umbrella will continually occupy your hands, which will prevent you from taking the necessary pictures. In such cases, a raincoat is very practical. You will be weatherproofed and able to take great pictures of Norway with your hands free thanks to it. In Norway, you may get raincoats in a variety of vibrant styles.

The nation's language problems

Be careful if you plan to stay in Norway because language barriers can be a big problem. There are many immigrants who contribute to the development of Norway's varied culture, and not every resident of the nation is fluent in English. If you intend to tour around the cities of Norway, we advise you to get along well with a local or a guide and bring them along with you. Other than the international citizens, the locals of Norway are more exposed to their native tongue. For instance, the elderly merchants, bus drivers, and other city transit drivers are largely uninitiated in English. Nevertheless, you won't face any major difficulties in Norway if you simply follow their linguistic cues. We also advise you to brush up on your language skills before traveling there. However, a substantial portion of Norwegians are literate in a basic level of English, which will make traveling around the nation very easy for you. Although the younger generation in Norway has more exposure to English, their skill in the language is not very high.

Norwegian cuisine

Norway's cuisine is exceptionally rich in tradition and culture. Many restaurants in Norway consistently put in a ton of effort to give visitors the most delectable cuisine that Norway has to offer. Although burgers and hot dogs tend to be among the top cuisines of Norway, street food culture is a very well-known culture that you can essentially avail of if you want to taste the best of Nordic Foods. You can visit any of the numerous restaurants in Norway's Oslo region to receive the best food. The most well-known restaurants in Norway are the Lysverket restaurant in Bergen and the Kontrast restaurant in the Oslo region. Both restaurants are well-liked internationally. Simply peruse the menu and keep an eye out for Norwegian specialties. Don't limit yourself to the country's burgers and hot dogs; sample the other options as well.

Avoid drawing comparisons to Sweden.

Although Sweden is a very cultured nation in Europe, according to Norwegians, that does not make it superior to Norway. When you are wandering the streets of Norway, at the very least, this must be your primary strategy. We advise you not to engage in any comparisons because the Norwegian people are quite sensitive about them and could further result in a disastrous situation. Although Sweden is less expensive than Norway as a whole, Norway is not less than Sweden. Wander the streets, take in the local culture, enjoy in the greatest cuisine a country has to offer, immerse yourself in its best traditions, and keep an eye out for opportunities to capture the best memories while exploring a new place.

Spend time in nature.

The best qualities Norway's nature has to offer are just waiting for you to catch up with them. In Norway, spring and summer are the greatest times to visit, and if you're traveling during those seasons, you may take advantage of the best seasonal treats. In Norway, the months of July through October are particularly captivating, and the nation is home to an abundance of berries, mushrooms, and other seasonal produce. Have everything you can, then choose the finest. The months of July through October seem to be the greatest for swimming at the numerous beaches. If you have a strong connection to nature, we advise you to take advantage of the numerous swimming facilities at this time. Skiing over the mountains, fishing in the country's many fjords, and enjoying the finest that Mother Nature has to give are some of the other most popular things to do at this season.

Money Problems

Forget about carrying cash if you're going to Norway. We advise you to avoid using cash in Norway because the locals there don't use it often. Norway's citizens do not accept the widespread use of cash since they are so concerned about many environmental hazards. Going cashless might be the greatest option if you want to travel safely in the nation. Doing so will prevent you from engaging in several safety risks when transacting money online, and you can also take advantage of other state perks. However, it's recommended to spend your money on train tickets rather than other forms of transportation because doing so will be quite advantageous for you because traveling around Norway by rail is very affordable. If you pay for your train tickets in cash, you will benefit, but be cautious when engaging in other activities because not all businesses accept cash.

Chapter 2: Facts About Norway

The Scandinavian region is home to the Nordic country of Norway, sometimes referred to as the Kingdom of Norway. You'll enjoy getting to know this nation, which is regarded as possibly Europe's most precipitous due to its stunning fjords and active population.

Before you start making travel arrangements for your ideal trip to Norway, a list of intriguing facts about the country might help you prepare. Get ready to fall in love with Norway the way we did!

1. The natural landscapes have an amazing variety.

You'll see a lot on a journey to Norway, from the fjords on the west coast to the snow-capped mountains. For instance, you may take a city break to explore Oslo's culture or go to the Arctic Circle. Even staying in a snow hotel is possible when seeing Norway in the winter.

One of Norway's most well-known places must be the western fjords. This area is said to have the highest number of fjords in the entire globe! Several of the country's well-known fjords include:

Listed by UNESCO, the world's most stunning fjord is Geirangerfjord.

Norway's longest and deepest fjord is called Sognefjord.

Nryfjord is a stop on the Norway in a Nutshell tour and a different fjord that is classified by UNESCO.

Pulpit Rock, one of Norway's most famous vistas, is located in Lysefjord.

More captivating natural wonders might be found at the Arctic Circle, where the magnificent archipelago of the Lofoten Islands is situated.

The region provides tourists the chance to wander along spotless beaches, take in the towering peaks of the skyline, and possibly even get a glimpse of the northern lights. Additionally, you can go wildlife viewing and learn about the region's Viking past.

2. It is possible to see polar bears in the wild

Naturally, you won't have to be concerned about this while navigating the streets of Oslo. However, the situation is somewhat different in isolated Svalbard.

One of the most northerly inhabited places on earth, Svalbard, is a true haven in the Arctic. The area in this region is protected by national parks, reserves, or sanctuaries in two thirds of its area. It is sometimes referred to as the "Realm of the Polar Bears" since there are more polar bears there than people.

The best Arctic location for wildlife viewing is Svalbard. You might observe seagulls, walruses, and whales in addition to the reindeer and Arctic fox, the archipelago's only native terrestrial species.

3. It ranks among the happiest nations in the world.

It is not surprising that Norway constantly ranks as one of the world's happiest countries in the World Happiness Report. The Happiness Research Institute in Denmark conducted the study, which demonstrates that the Nordic region is not only aesthetically beautiful but also a happy location.

Numerous additional yearly evaluations, such as the Global Peace Index, state that Norway is a safe and tranquil location to visit. Oslo also serves as the location for the yearly awarding of the Nobel Peace Prize.

Given their abundance of magnificent natural beauty and enjoyment of the great outdoors, it is not surprising that the Norwegians are contented people. So why not visit Norway and experience it firsthand?

4. A hop-on, hop-off cruise around the coast is offered.

One of the most beautiful and rocky coastlines on earth is found in Norway, which spans over three seas: the North Sea, Norwegian Sea, and Barents Sea. Fortunately, it's one of the easiest to discover thanks to the Hurtigruten Coastal Voyage.

You will travel almost 1,255 kilometers in one direction on this historic trip from Kirkenes in the north to Bergen in the south (780 miles).

The trip takes about 6 to 7 days, though you are not forced to complete it in that time frame. You can even join the cruise for a certain leg or get off along the way to see different places. Along the journey, you may take tours of Trondheim, the Lofoten Islands, and Norway's North Cape.

This is the best way to go about spending time touring the Norwegian west coast.

5. The sun never sets in the summer.

The midnight sun is something to take advantage of if you visit northern Norway in the summer. Enjoy the surroundings at night while the sun is shining since there will be more daylight for outdoor activities and a more local way of life.

For instance, from May to July, the sun only sets in the northern city of Troms for three to five hours each night. Additionally, June, which is closer to the summer solstice, has no sundown at all.

A sleeping mask is a necessity if you're traveling right now.

6. Its capital is a major hub for contemporary art.

In Oslo, the Norwegian capital, you may find a blend of traditional Scandinavian style and contemporary influences. It should be at the top of your list because it is a thriving center for art and culture if you want to learn about contemporary Norwegian artists.

Explore the many art galleries in the city to gain a taste of this intriguing world. The Munch Museum, the Norwegian National Gallery, and the area around Aker Brygge Wharf are top choices for history and culture.

You might find it interesting to know that the Norwegian King and Queen, as well as the royal family, reside at the Royal Palace in Oslo.

7. The best road excursions in the world may be found in Norway.

There are many common ways to travel around Norway, including by train and boat. However, deciding to drive will guarantee that you have the trip of a lifetime.

So why not travel through Norway on your own schedule? Not only may you go at your own pace, but you can also stop whenever you wish to admire the scenery.

Furthermore, you may drive with confidence on Norwegian roads because they have some of the best safety rules in the world.

8. You can look for the aurora borealis.

One of the best places in the world to see the northern lights is Norway. Northern Norway is actually in the heart of the "aurora zone" or "northern lights belt." This band's auroral frequency and intensity, which circle the Earth, are widely known.

If you want to see the northern lights for yourself, make sure you visit the north during the winter. There are apps that can help you check the weather conditions as well.

We suggest avoiding populated regions in search of places with less light pollution. In remote areas like the Lofoten Islands, Troms, and Svalbard, you'll have a good chance of seeing the aurora if the weather is favorable.

The northern lights are normally most active between the hours of 11 PM and 2 AM, so if you're serious about seeing the aurora, you should stay up late.

9. Norwegian cuisine is delectable.

When you think of Norwegian cuisine, perhaps nothing in particular comes to mind. But we're sure you'll enjoy discovering it. In the towns and cities of the nation, there are a lot of trendy modern eateries that place an emphasis on regional and seasonal cuisine.

As you might expect, Norwegian seafood is deliciously fresh. Did you know that salmon sushi was created in Norway? The most northerly sushi restaurant on earth is in Svalbard, so you might even decide to visit there.

Furthermore, you'll find that breakfast differs from country to country, including Australia, Canada, and the United States. In general, savory dishes receive more attention. Regional favorites include rye bread, cheese, pig, and smoked or pickled fish. Don't forget to try brunost, a popular brown whey cheese from Norway, while you're on vacation.

10. Norwegian rail journeys are regarded as the best in Europe.

One of the best ways to travel in Scandinavia is by rail. Additionally, you'll be treated to various excursions throughout Norway with stunning scenery. The Flam railway, which is recognized as one of the most beautiful railways in the entire world, is among the most well-known lines.

If you decide to go by train, you may relax and take in the landscape. For instance, you can observe glittering fjords and craggy mountain peaks without getting up from your seat when traveling from Oslo to Bergen.

Chapter 3:
Key Places To Visit In Norway

Even the straightforward word of Norway conjures us images of vast fjords, the spectacular northern lights, winding mountain roads, and valiant Vikings. If you're considering visiting Norway to explore its towns, wilderness, and landmarks, where should you go?

This Nordic country boasts an abundance of attractive sites and is renowned for its extraordinary natural beauty. This area is home to fjords, waterfalls, hiking trails, small communities hidden beneath massive mountains, and vibrant cities.

To help you narrow down your bucket list, we've produced this list of Norway's top attractions. Continue reading and pick a few (or all!) to build your enchanted Norway itinerary.

1. The Oslo region

The lavish capital of Norway, Oslo, is a popular tourist destination, particularly for short city breaks or to experience Norwegian culture. Along with its fascinating past and attractions, it benefits from a "small town" atmosphere thanks to its lovely waterfront and the surrounding natural surroundings.

You'll see a lovely combination of both traditional Scandinavian style and modern metro influences during your trip. Take it all in while strolling through the center of the city and making stops at the sights you want to see.

You may stroll around the harbor and see Aker Brygge and the Akershus Fortress. The Oslo Cathedral is a short stroll from the Royal Palace. The Munch Museum is a great place to get some art. At Frogner Park, you can discover a number of sculptures by renowned Norwegian artist Gustav Vigeland.

Visit the Bygdoy peninsula via short ferry to learn more about early Norway's history and see real Viking ships. Here is where the Norwegian Museum of Cultural History and the Fram Museum are situated.

2. The Iconic Pulpit Rock

Pulpit Rock, also known as "Preikestolen" in Norwegian, is yet another must-see landmark in that country. Its name derives from its shape, which is a vertical cliff with a flat top that resembles a pulpit. Because of the gorgeous surroundings and stunning views from the top, it has become one of Norway's most popular walks.

This day trip in Stavanger in southwest Norway is ideal if you're looking for excitement. You will need to climb up a challenging 3.8 kilometer (2.4 mile) trail with an elevation gain of around 334 meters in about 2 hours (1,096 feet). The summit will welcome you with stunning views of the mountains and fjords.

If you're a serious hiker or exploring the western fjords, you shouldn't skip the other must-do hike, Trolltunga, which is close to Bergen.

3. The western fjords and Geirangerfjord

When you think about Norway, you might envision vast fjords, rough mountains, and gushing waterfalls. Visit the western fjords if that's what you're looking for.

You should visit Geirangerfjord, one of the most beautiful fjords in the world, as said previously. It features picturesque scenery with clear waters, towering hills, and a wide diversity of vegetation. Here are the waterfalls known as Seven Sisters and Bridal Veil.

The Seven Sisters waterfall is named for its seven separate streams, the largest of which is 250 meters high (820 feet). According to local folklore, the Friaren (The Suitor) is said to be enamored of the "sisters" from the opposite side of the fjord as they joyfully dance on the mountain.

Detailed information on what to see and do in one of Norway's most stunning spots can be found in our guide to Geirangerfjord.

You might also visit other fjords in Norway, such Sognefjord, which is the longest and deepest fjord in the entire world. More than 200 kilometers (124 miles) of it are located inland from Bergen on the west coast.

The smallest fjord in Norway, Naeroyfjord, a branch of Sognefjord, should not be overlooked. Along with Geirangerfjord, it was listed as a UNESCO World Heritage Site in 2005.

4. Modest Bergen

Visit Bergen on Norway's west coast to get a sense of the country's culture, history, and landscape. The second-largest city in Norway, Bergen, is recognized for being the "Gateway to the Fjords." You can take some day trips to the fjords if you're visiting this area for a city break.

Bryggen, another World Heritage Site in Norway, is situated in Bergen. This 900-year-old dock, which is also one of the city's most well-liked attractions, is actually the oldest portion of Bergen. Given how vibrant it is, you cannot possible miss it.

As you meander along the crowded cobblestone pathways, discover more about Bergen's role as the Hanseatic league's capital. The multicolored wooden buildings were painstakingly restored to its original medieval features following a terrible fire in the 1700s.

For further history, you might also visit the newly rebuilt Fantoft Stave Church, which dates back to 1150.

In search of those expansive vistas of the city and the ocean? Climb one of the city's seven surrounding mountains. As an alternative, you could ride the Floibanen funicular railway up to Mount Floyen. Mount Ulriken can also be reached by cable car.

5. The town of Flam

You may enjoy a scenic train ride from Oslo to the fjords by taking the Flamsbana (Flam railway). From the Myrdal mountain station, board this tiny green train and travel 20 kilometers (12 miles). Look out the window as you plunge 865 meters (2,837 ft) into the breathtaking Flam Valley.

It is in reality regarded as one of the most beautiful railways in the entire world. Stops in the fjords and Flam can be included in a Norway in a Nutshell tour.

The tiny town of Flam is a favourite destination for nature lovers because of its deep valleys, thundering waterfalls, and steep mountain sides. Just a few of the attractions in this area include the 17th-century Flam Church and the Flamsbana Museum, which is close to the train station.

From here, you can take walks, kayaking excursions, and boat cruises to observe the local flora and scenery.

6. Stylish Alesund

The harbor city of Alesund is located on Norway's west coast around midway between Bergen and Trondheim. Alesund, which is surrounded by numerous connected islands, provides a taste of living by the sea. On a wildlife viewing cruise, this is the place to go if you're a devoted bird watcher.

Most people probably associate the town with its Art Nouveau structures. Alesund had to be almost entirely rebuilt after being completely destroyed by fire in the early 20th century. Discover the bustling downtown and take in the fresh architecture.

Another reason to take a side trip or city break to Alesund is its proximity to Geirangerfjord. Explore Norway's most famous fjord from here. Lesund is a favorite stop on the Hurtigruten coastal cruise.

For the greatest views of the town and the surrounding archipelago, head to the Mount Aksla viewpoint.

8. The islands of Lofoten

Norway has a huge range of topography. This means that you might take a trip up north to view the Arctic Circle in addition to visiting the towns in the south and the fjords in the west.

The Lofoten archipelago in northern Norway is renowned for its breathtaking natural landscape, little fishing villages, and outstanding lighting that is ideal for photography.

Svolvaer serves as both the harbor and the city of Lofoten. There are shops, cafes, and art galleries there. On the horizon, you can see the Svolvaer Goat ("Svolvaergeita") mountain, a favorite of rock climbers.

There are two other settlements in the archipelago that you could visit: Reine and Henningsvr. Both of them are near the ocean, with towering mountains rising dramatically in the background.

Another really well-liked pastime on these islands is nature observation. The waterways are teeming with marine life, and it's possible to observe otters, seals, and whales there.

9. The coast of the Arctic

Learn more about Arctic Norway by exploring the region's northern shore on foot or by boat.

The region of northern Norway, which stretches from Tromso to Kirkenes and passes via the North Cape, is spectacular. In Tromso, commonly referred to as the "Paris of the North," see the Arctic Cathedral and take the Fjellheisen cable car up to Storsteinen for wide views of the surroundings.

The North Cape is the northernmost point of Europe. That's one to put on your bucket list.

Kirkenes is the last stop on a seashore journey. Due to its proximity to Finland and Russia's borders, it is an excellent place to learn about the Sami people and experience Arctic experiences. The town of Kirkenes is home to the legendary SnowHotel.

No of the season, finding this place is a treasure. Enjoy limitless days of adventures, adventurous hikes, and boat cruises in the summertime. In the other half of the year, you could look forward to a winter wonderland and snowy activities.

Of course, one of the best parts of visiting this far north between October and March is witnessing the northern lights. This time of year, when polar nights occur in the Arctic Circle, offers the best opportunities to witness nature's most spectacular light display.

10. Svalbard

Do you want to go on a longer arctic adventure? Travel to the Svalbard archipelago, which is situated halfway between mainland Norway and the North Pole.

It is one of the most northern places on earth where people live and is also home to polar bears. Indeed, they outnumber humanity in number! Here, one may marvel at the majestic glaciers and the vast, uninhabited Arctic tundra.

Chapter 4: Tourists Attraction Sites

1.Oslo

The city of Oslo is icy, traditional, and exorbitantly pricey. So how does it continue to be ranked as one of the top cities in the world? The largest and capital city of Norway blooms in the summer. Every street will come alive on a warm summer day as the city's charm comes to light. People are gathered in leafy parks to relax on the lush grass, while children's laughing fills the air. Friends are catching up at cafes, restaurants are bustling, and live music can be heard everywhere coming from side streets.

History & Culture

The city of Oslo was founded about the year 1000 and was an important trading center for the huge Viking Empire. The name Oslo is derived from "Old Norse," and although its exact meaning is unknown, it is believed to relate to a meadow. Oslo has experienced significant upheaval throughout its existence as a city a few times.

Three-quarters of Oslo's population perished in the Black Plague in 1350, and the city was completely destroyed by two large fires in the 1600s. Norway's strength waned throughout this time, which of course also affected its capital city. Norway was bound to its neighbors, who were afterwards dominated by Sweden after Denmark at first.

In spite of everything, the city bounced back, powerful and together. Due to its strategic waterfront location, it has historically served as a major center for marine activities. There are currently offices for many of the biggest shipping corporations in the globe.

About 650 000 people currently live in Oslo, and this number is growing quickly. It is today one of the largest cities in Europe with the quickest growth, partly as a result of new immigrants. The diverse population of Oslo only serves to enhance the distinctive atmosphere of the city. The city's culture is enhanced by a huge and dazzling array of art galleries and museums, and the city's numerous outdoor sculptures pique the wanderer's interest.

Vigeland Park

Attractions & Activities

Favorite ship museums include the Kon-Tiki Museum and the Viking Ship Museum, which has a collection of longboats. The polar ship "Fram" that transported Roald Amundsen to Antarctica for his historic trip to the South Pole in 1911 is visible here.

Without seeing at least a portion of Oslo's 2600km of ski slopes and cross-country trails during the winter, a trip would not be complete. This is where the Holmenkollen Ski Jump, which opened in 1892 and is now a museum, is the oldest of Norway's icy slopes. Although the view from the top of the drop is disorienting, you can also visit the tower's observation deck.

Visit St Hanshaugen park, one of Oslo's biggest parks, for a stroll on a beautiful sunny day. Due to its past as a location for Midsummer's celebrations, this park is fascinating.

Make sure to visit the Vigeland Sculpture Park if the sculptures in the city have captured your attention. More than 200 statues made of bronze, granite, and iron are shown there. The Little Angry Boy and the Wheel of Life are two of the most well-known sculptures, so be sure to see them.

The Fjords

The magnificent feeling you get when you first stand in awe and look down upon Norway's Fjords cannot be put into words. Due to its untamed, rugged beauty, the west of the country has received UNESCO World Heritage classification. This is a result of the region's distinctive landscape.

Even though you might be tempted to continue gazing at the first fjord you come across, it is actually imperative that you travel to a number of the magnificent strands that make up the network of fjords in order to fully comprehend their majesty.

All tourists to Norway must investigate the historical remnants that the long and rich history of Norway's Fjords has left behind. As you learn about the stave churches, Viking history, and codfish trade, be amazed.

It is crucial to understand that the fjords span a wide area and that access to many of them is prohibited owing to ice buildup for the most of the winter as well as during inclement weather. However, there are a number of historical sites and structures in the area that help to narrate stories from the previous millennium.

Agatunet, a designated hamlet close to the Hardangerfjord, has 30 structures that date from the Middle Ages to the present. Both a changing art display and an exhibition of traditional costumes are available. It's always a fantastic family day out when they host weaving and baking demos over the summer.

Geirangerfjord

The Geirangerfjord is a beautiful expanse of deep blue that looks as though it were carved out of soaring rock faces. Despite being one of the tiniest, it is unquestionably one of the most stunning fjords. In the summer, boats depart from a charming tiny hamlet with a wooden pier on the eastern end of the island. You can anticipate seeing waterfalls tumbling into the fjord's depths and marveling at dolphins playing in the waves created by passing boats. Even the scenic, full of unusual vistas "Eagle's Highway" road to Geiranger that zigzags across the mountains.

The world's smallest fjord, Naeroyfjord, is to the south. You can kayak across the emerald-green waterways and glide over the glassy surface while listening to silence in this area to get up close and personal with the waters and the fauna.

Other activities available in Norway's Fjords include cycling, hiking, and fishing. Scaling the blue-tinged Nigardsbreen Glacier is another option for those adrenaline junkies looking for the height of exhilaration. For those with more time, this amazing trip is located a little farther inland from the fjords.

2. Bergen

Bergen is undoubtedly one of Norway's most picturesque cities and is frequently referred to as the "Gateway to the Fjords." It is acknowledged as the nation's cultural capital and was honored as the 2000 European City of Culture.

Bergen is a large city with a small-town charm and an ambiance that, despite the chilly weather, warms the hearts of those who visit. It is full of history and tradition. The best way to see Bergen is on foot. The city's charm is enhanced by its cobblestone streets and winding passageways dotted with wooden cottages.

Culture and History

In the past, Bergen was a significant hub for marine trade. Due to this, the city attracted the merchants who constructed and maintained the wooden Bryggen, or old wharf, buildings. The red, white, and yellow houses of the Bryggen, which are now a UNESCO World Heritage site, are immaculately kept and constantly busy. With its chic cafes, smart galleries, and little stores, this is the place to go for an afternoon stroll.

One of Norway's most popular outdoor marketplaces, the scenic and bustling Fish Market, gives visitors a true sense of Bergen culture. In addition to selling fruit, vegetables, flowers, handicrafts, and souvenirs, it boasts a picturesque setting in the middle of the city between the fjords and Bergen's seven mountains.

Music lovers might like to go to the residence of composer Edvard Grieg (1843-1907). Grieg spent 22 years living here and creating many of his most well-known pieces in the tiny garden house. His contributions to the musical arts are still honored today.

Fløibanen

Attractions & Activities

The Flibanen funicular train is one of Bergen's most well-known landmarks. Just 150 meters away from Bryggen in the city center, the journey begins. Getting to the top of Mount Flyen is an adventure in and of itself, and those who love the outdoors will find hiking routes and gorgeous surroundings there.

If that's still not enough for you, the Ulriken Panoramic Tour transports you by double-decker bus and cable car to the highest of Bergen's renowned "Seven Mountains," which rises 642m above the city streets. Beautiful views of Bergen and the surrounding sea, islands, fjords, and mountains can be seen from the summit.

The Bergen Aquarium is a well-liked gathering spot for both locals and tourists. Watching all the strange and fascinating things that occur below the surface can keep you occupied for hours. You can meet additional animals including crocodiles, snakes, and lizards in addition to learning about the cod and the other wildlife that inhabit the Norwegian shore.

Finally, and most significantly, ask the information desk which of the fjord trips is best for your stay at that particular time of year. You can choose from a variety of wonderful cruises with varying lengths to make the trip fit your preferences.

3. Tromso

The largest and busiest town in Northern Norway is Tromso, which is located over 400 kilometers above the Arctic Circle. Despite this, the Gulf Stream's warmer air currents help to temper the town's climate a little.

Its surrounding halo of snow-capped mountains offers stunning views all year long and offers wonderful hiking and skiing opportunities. The never-ending brilliance of the summer days counterbalances the winter's seemingly endless darkness. If you want to celebrate the midnight sun, come here.

Culture and History

There is evidence that Tromso was inhabited as long ago as 9000 years ago. However, its extensive history dates back to roughly 850 AD. Tromso, a town with a sizable Norse and Sami background, has long been a notable town due to its advantageous location. Tromso rose to prominence as the principal town for Arctic hunting in the 1820s. You may learn more about this at the Polar Museum.

Today, Tromso is a vibrant city with cultural events, buskers, a bustling street scene, a marathon at midnight, a reputable university, and more bars per resident than any other town in Norway.

The 11 arcing triangles of the 1965 Arctic Cathedral are arguably Tromso's most famous landmark. Tromsdalen Church is the name given to it formally. The vast and exquisite stained-glass window shows Christ coming down to earth, while the design shows glacial crevasses and auroral curtains. Pay attention to the crystal lamps created in Czech Republic; they resemble icicles hanging in midair.

The Arctic Cathedral

Attractions & Activities

Take the cable car to Mt. Storsteinen's 421m summit for a beautiful view of the city and the midnight sun. At the peak, there is a restaurant from which a network of celestial hiking trails radiates.

Join a husky safari for a quick journey into the far-off, snowy wilderness if you're looking for a truly unique experience. Near Tromso, there are a number of husky farms where you may meet and engage with the curious huskies. You have the option of sitting inside or operating your 2-person sled as you race around the stunning Kvalya Island's white winter beauty. Refuel with a delectable Sami supper in a "lavvo," a tepee-like tent, back at the husky farm while you take advantage of the Norwegian hospitality.

A viewing excursion departing from Tromso is an option if you're eager to see the Northern Lights. Replace the city's electric lighting with the surrounding, pitch-black wilderness. If you look up at the stars while sitting next to a roaring campfire, you might be lucky enough to see a show that you'll never forget.

4.Trondheim

Originally serving as Norway's capital, Trondheim is currently the third-largest city in the nation (after Oslo and Bergen). It's a genuinely attractive city with broad streets and a mostly pedestrianized center.

The city is teeming with educational institutions, notably St. Olav's University Hospital and the renowned Norwegian University of Science and Technology. Due to the high student population, Trondheim is a vibrant city. Trondheim now offers a lifestyle that you can really kick back and enjoy for a few days. Add to the mix some outstanding cafes and restaurants, as well as a number of excellent museums.

Culture and History

When the Viking Age began in the year 997, Trondheim was established as a trading center and remained Norway's capital until 1217. It has also gone by the names Kaupangen, Nidaros, and Trondhjem in the past.

In the city's history, there have been ten significant fires. The dwellings were all made of wood, so the fires did a lot of damage. In fact, the fire in 1651 destroyed 90% of all the structures inside the city borders. The city was nearly completely rebuilt only 30 years after the fire in 1681, also known as the Horneman Fire.

In response to the flames, a law was created requiring wide streets throughout the town, which are still present today. To stop the fires from spreading as they have in the past, they were to serve as barriers.

Nazi Germany controlled Trondheim during World War II from April 9, 1940, when Norway was invaded, to May 8, 1945, when the war in Europe came to a close. It was a significant submarine station at the time, and it has remained a significant shipping town over time.

Nidaros Cathedral

Attractions & Activities

During the occupation of Norway during World War II, the 13th U-boat Flotilla was housed at DORA 1, a German submarine facility. The city archives, as well as the university and state archives, are among the many archives that are currently housed in the bunker. DORA has also served as a concert venue more recently.

The House of Rock must be passed by by music lovers. This fantastic museum honors mostly Norwegian musicians from the 1950s to the present and is focused on pop and rock music. Given that many of Norway's most well-known and successful musicians hail from this trendy city, Trondheim, its location is suitable. Visitors can stand in wonder and stare up at the enormous projecting roof that rises above an equally enormous converted warehouse and features Norwegian record covers.

The Nidaros Cathedral is the most significant Gothic structure in Norway and, during the Middle Ages, it served as the primary Christian pilgrimage destination for all of Northern Europe. Even though it took several years, construction began in 1070. The shrine now stands over the ancient burial of St. Olav, a Viking ruler who introduced Christianity to the Nordic pagan religion.

5. Lofoten

The group of islands known as Lofoten are located in the Arctic Circle. They are a treasure in a way that is exceptional in the world because of their breathtaking beauty. As you approach the islands on the ferry, they appear desolate from a distance. Sharp rocks protrude from the ocean, and the coastline is rough with several vertical cliff faces.

Then, as you go closer and take a closer look, you'll see that every island within the fjords has picture-perfect fishing communities and stunning bays. The cleanest air you can find is in the fresh arctic air.

The Lofoten archipelago is located near Greenland and northern Alaska at a similar latitude. Due to the Gulf Stream's movement, it has a comparatively milder climate, and summertime highs of 23C are not unusual. In spite of this, you should be aware that even in the summer, the weather can change fast and become chilly at any time.

Culture and History

Through fish exports, this coastal region has historically made significant contributions to national prosperity. We know this because the largest chiefdom from the Viking Age ever discovered was recently uncovered during archaeological investigations. Visit the museums and take a journey through the region's 9000 years to learn more.

A new motorway that connected the islands to the mainland for the first time opened in 2007. That implies that taking a ferry to get there is no longer required. Nearly as breathtaking as the view at the destination is the harsh scenery along the route. This drive has been designated as a National Trust Drive, and it also borders the Moysanen National Park.

Lofoten's Houses Built on Stilts

Attractions & Activities

Despite its spectacular scenery, Lofoten is a well-liked destination for cyclists since it has a lot of flat territory. The numerous side streets and well-maintained roads can lead the intrepid traveler to a number of tiny fishing communities. These islands' distinctive views, like the wooden drying racks stuffed with cod, contribute to their allure. In addition to being able to join a tour group, cycling equipment can be rented.

In the Lofoten town of Laukvik, visit the Polarlight Centre for a fascinating and instructive experience. A vibrant presentation of the Northern Lights is provided by the center and lasts for about an hour. The staff is there to answer any questions you may have. During your entire stay in Lofoten, the center offers a unique feature that lets you sign up for text message alerts when the Northern Lights are visible.

Kayaking vacations are also very popular in the Lofoten archipelago. For kayakers of every skill level, a number of local businesses provide year-round guided tours and trips. If you want to advance your kayaking skills, more seasoned kayakers have the option of attending a longer sea kayaking trip lasting several days or a technique course.

6.Stavanger

Southern Norway's Stavanger is a town with an intriguing blend of modern industry and old-world charm. The busy harbor is lined with historic dockside warehouses, and the evenings are lively, especially during the hotter summer months. The city offers a diverse range of cultural experiences, while the surrounding Norwegian landscape still charms those who enjoy being outside.

Culture and History

The Stavanger cathedral was finished in 1125, which is considered the city of Stavanger's official founding year. The majority of the wooden homes in Stavanger's historic district date from the 18th and 19th centuries and are now protected as a part of the city's cultural history. Due to this, the inner city and town center (Gamle Stavanger) have maintained the majority of its small-town charm, which always draws tourists to the area.

The city has seen economic booms and busts continuously throughout its history. The most significant industries throughout history have been shipping, shipbuilding, fishing, and fish canning. A fresh boom began in 1969 when oil was discovered for the first time in the North Sea.

Following the establishment of Stavanger as the on-shore oil industry's hub, there was a period of rapid expansion. Today, Stavanger is regarded as Norway's oil industry's hub and one of Europe's energy capitals. It is also frequently referred to as Europe's oil capital.

Gamle Stavanger

Attractions & Activities

The Stavanger Concert Hall serves as the area's primary cultural hub. The concert hall boasts a dynamic and varied program that features activities all year long. A trip to the orchestra hall is definitely worthwhile because hearing a symphony orchestra perform there is amazing.

Exhibits at the Norwegian Petroleum Museum detail the origins, discoveries, production, and applications of oil and gas. This museum will interest visitors of all ages, and a 3D theater nearby also shows a feature film continuously. The museum also offers information on technological developments and the impact of oil on Norwegian culture. The North Sea Divers, along with the risks involved in their line of work and the difficulties they face, are the subject of an especially intriguing new exhibit.

Take the bus from Stavanger to Hafrsfjord to witness the "Swords in Rock" monument, which will immerse you in Viking history. In 872 AD, a battle took place here that resulted in the unification of Norway into a single monarchy. The monument stands for harmony, freedom, and peace. The swords used by the Vikings are replicas of weapons that have been discovered across the nation.

7. Alesund

Alesund is in a picturesque location nestled between the towering Sunnmore Mountains and the gushing fjords. Visitors with an interest in architecture can find a lot of structures that are quite attractive to the eye in this city, which is renowned for its Art Nouveaux building style. It is without a doubt in part because of the numerous turrets, spires, and exquisite ornamentation on the building facades that it was chosen as Norway's most beautiful town in 2007 and 2009.

Culture and History

The city of Alesund was consumed by a horrific fire on a chilly January morning in 1904. Ten thousand people were made homeless and 850 homes were completely destroyed in the course of 16 hours. Nevertheless, this tragic occurrence gave rise to new life, and the town was remodeled and rebuilt in the Art Nouveau style.

Visit the farm where Ivar Aasen resided in the 1800s if you are truly interested in learning more about the history of the Norwegian language. He is credited with developing the Nynorsk (New Norwegian) language. The Ivar Aasen Center is a national documentation and experience center for Nynorsk literary culture and is devoted to Aasen's life's work. The structure itself is an intriguing draw.

If your vacation occurs to overlap with the festival dates, the Festival of New Norwegian Literature, Art, and Music is held here every year during the last week of June and is a fantastic way to spend a few hours.

Alnes Lighthouse

Attractions & Activities

Life under the sea is on exhibit at the Atlantic Sea Park, one of Scandinavia's largest aquariums, for a fun and instructive trip for kids. Don't overlook the neighboring locations, which are easily accessible if Alesund is your base of operations, despite the fact that Alesund boasts a variety of activities and sights that are well worth seeing.

Visit Runde, a little island invaded each year by more than 500,000 breeding birds, which is located on the southernmost bird cliff in Norway. This bird refuge is home to more than 220 species, including the common and adorable puffins.

Godoy Island's environs provide stunning and diverse walking landscape, including both clean beaches and towering mountains. You can purchase artwork at Alnes Lighthouse to keep as a memento or to bring home as gifts. In the summer, visitors can take a guided tour of this protected lighthouse.

Fjords and mountains in Sunnmre provide the ideal setting for a special and enjoyable family winter experience. There are lots of wonderful cross-country skiing trails to select from. There are uninhabited mountains where skilled explorers can occasionally ski all the way from the mountain tops down to the fjord.

Preikestolen

Preikestolen, a place of breathtaking natural beauty only 25 kilometers from Stavanger, has drawn tourists for years. A nearly square rock structure protrudes from the surrounding mountainside far above Lysefjorden.

This amazing sandstone terrace, which is only 25 by 25 meters, climbs 604 meters above Lysefjorden. It is one of the most well-liked tourist spots in Norway with an astounding 200,000 visitors annually.

The name of the rocky outcropping was Hyvlatonn when it was first mentioned. Interestingly, that means "planned tooth" in English. The local tourism association, which intended to promote the area as a trekking destination, was responsible for the adoption of the name Preikestolen around the turn of the 20th century.

The English translation of Preikestolen's present name is Preacher's Rock, also known as Pulpit Rock. This is due to the fact that many people think the rock is similar to a preacher's pulpit, elevated as he addresses the people gathered below.

The trail leading to Preikestolen has recently undergone spectacular improvement work thanks to a group of expert stonemasons, many of whom are from Nepal. To lessen the environmental effect caused by the numerous visitors each year, steps have been constructed in the toughest parts and a rocky route has been created.

Since there are no obstacles or fencing along the pathway, extreme caution must be exercised when using it. When determining whether to go on this walk with young children, take this into account.

Trail for Hiking to Preikestolen

The path ascends to a height of 604 meters from its starting point at Preikestolhytta, which is 270 meters above sea level. The hiking track is only 3.8 kilometers long in each direction. Although the majority of people may now now enjoy the sights of Preikestolen thanks to the new and better pathway, it takes about 2 hours, depending on the experience and fitness levels of the hikers.

Remember that the accumulation of snow and ice in the winter and spring can make the track slick. Although you will still need the proper boots, the best time to trek the trail is from April through October.

There are a few easy alternatives for people who can't complete the walk or would rather not hike. From June through August, a summertime tourist ferry runs from Lauvvik to Lysebotn and passes directly beneath Pulpit Rock. But as this is a well-traveled road, making reservations far in advance is advised. The Lysefjord can be navigated by ship, which is a more expensive alternative.

National Park of Jotunheimen

250 peaks make up the huge mountain range known as Jotunheimen National Park, some of which soar more than 2000 meters into the sky. With a wide variety of winter and summer activities available, it is a well-liked destination for tourists because of its accessible location between Oslo, Bergen, and Trondheim. The highest mountain range in northern Europe is also home to untamed species and is surrounded by pristine wilderness and breathtaking scenery.

In Jotunheimen National Park, evidence of human settlement from 3000 years ago has been found. Elk, reindeer, and trout were essential foods that helped the earliest Norwegian inhabitants survive and prosper in these stunning mountain ranges.

They only left behind fishing hooks, spears, fish traps, and trapping equipment. The countryside is entirely untouched, and as it has been protected as a National Park since 1980, the flora, animals, and wildlife have been permitted to grow.

Jotunheimen is home to all four species of deer (reindeer, roe deer, red deer, and elk), as well as wolverine, lynx, and arctic foxes. Naturally, there is a large variety of bird life, and their lovely melodies of freedom and delight fill the crisp mountain air.

Across the years, Jotunheimen has become more and more accessible; ski paths are now clearly designated, and a number of unmanned huts and cabins have been built all over the park, allowing people to camp or remain overnight shielded from the erratic weather.

National Park of Jotunheimen

Whatever your specialty or passion, Jotunheimen is a haven for outdoor explorers. The park is traversed by glaciers that are like enormous wedges of crystal, and the rivers are raging with white rapids that are just waiting to carry thrill-seekers into the unknown. Waterfalls roar in the heart of the park's serene Zen.

The mountains offer difficult climbs for mountain climbers, and there are more than 300km of routes waiting to take hikers and cyclists into breathtakingly beautiful landscapes. Anyone who wants to climb the highest mountains will need specialized equipment and a climbing guide.

For overnight stays, there is a lodging choice for any preference. You can stay in the height of luxury at one of the boutique hotels, tent out in complete seclusion, or bunk up in a simple log cabin.

Fishing and hunting are permitted, but licenses must be obtained in advance, and there are other regulations that must be followed to protect the area's natural beauty.

Lillehammer

The late 19th-century collection of wooden homes that make up Lillehammer's town center are in a magnificent site overlooking the northern shore of Lake Mjsa and the river Lgen. It is the perfect vacation spot for anyone looking for incredible outdoor adventures because it is surrounded by mountains and located in the center of Norway.

The village is close to the Rondane, Jotunheimen, and Langsua National Parks, which offer some of the nation's most breathtaking landscape. There are also many intriguing museums and attractions to visit for a cultural treat or to pass the time on a gloomy day.

Culture and History

Since the Norwegian Iron Age, the area has been inhabited, and by the 1800s, Lillehammer had a bustling market. Despite its tiny size and quiet atmosphere, the town played host to the Lillehammer affair in 1973, in which Israeli Mossad agents mistakenly shot and murdered a Moroccan waiter.

On a happier note, Lillehammer held the Winter Olympics in 1994 and will hold the Winter Youth Olympics in 2016. Visitor access is available to all of the Olympic-use arenas. Then, in 2005, the well-known British motor program Top Gear aired its "Winter Olympics special." It was an episode featuring several automobile challenges with Olympic themes that took place in the areas of Lillehammer.

In unrelated pop culture, Lillehammer is the setting for the 2012 American TV series "Lilyhammer." In the show, a New York gangster relocates to Lillehammer under the Witness Protection Program after being motivated to do so by the 1994 Winter Olympics.

Maihaugen Open-Air Museum

Attractions & Activities

As previously indicated, Lillehammer's Olympic past is still very much present, and all of the venues used for the various events are accessible to the general public. Visit the Norwegian Olympic Museum, the only one of its kind in

Europe, to discover more about Olympic history from 1896 to the present.

In close proximity to Lillehammer, the Maihaugen Open-Air Museum offers a glimpse into life and work in Norway over the previous 50 years. To enjoy culture indoors, visit the Lillehammer Art Museum. The numerous pieces on show by well-known Norwegian artists like Fritz Thaulow and Edvard Munch will be appreciated by visitors.

There are 5 ski resorts nearby, and Hunderfossen Family Park is a local amusement park. There are countless chances for equestrian riding, cycling, skiing, and hiking. Lillehammer is a haven for any busy young family with so many things to do, and your next adventure is never far away.

Kristiansand

Kristiansand, located at the extreme southernmost point of Norway, is a region that is becoming more and more notable in terms of its historical findings.

As a royal residence, Danish-Norwegian stronghold, and subsequently garrison town, Kristiansand has always been significant from a military and geopolitical standpoint. Even today, with a frequent ferry connection to Denmark, Kristiansand serves as a gateway to and from the continent of Europe.

Culture and History

King Christian IV, who established the city in 1641, was honored with its name. Sand, the second component, alludes to the sandy headland on which the city was founded. Contrary to appearances, the Kristiansand region has been inhabited for a very long time. An ancient woman's well-preserved skeleton from around 6500 BC was found nearby in 1996.

Rural communities from many centuries ago were found by archaeological digs to the east of Oddernes Church. Other finds in nearby grave mounds appear to support the theory that occupancy started around 400 AD. Additionally, 25 cooking pits that were probably even older were discovered right outside the chapel wall.

Grave discoveries from a few years ago indicated that the churchyard may have already been abnormally vast in the Middle Ages. This implies that the region must have had a sizable population before the Black Death decimated it. Kristiansand is an interesting location for both historians and archaeologists since it has so much history and so much evidence that is continuously being found.

Kristiansand Zoo

Attractions & Activities

A sizable zoo and theme park called the Kristiansand Zoo can be found 11 kilometers to the east of Kristiansand. The attraction has five distinct parks: a zoo, a water park, a theme park, a forest park, and an entertainment park. It is one of the only sites in the world where you may view the red panda, which is currently threatened with extinction, and animals have wide, open regions in which to wander.

The undiscovered jewel of Kristiansand is Ravnedalen, a lush, tranquil setting where guests may unwind on the lawn, explore the trees, and watch swans drifting across the dam's waters. There is a café with tasty food that is also a well-liked location for summertime concerts.

A short distance from Kristiansand, along the coast, is where you'll find the Grnningen Lighthouse. It was operational from 1878 until 1980, when it switched to automation. In 1994, the lighthouse was designated as a heritage structure and is now accessible to tourists. Even overnight accommodations at the lighthouse can be arranged during the summer for a truly one-of-a-kind experience.

Longyearbyen

Despite only having 2000 residents, Longyearbyen is the Norwegian Svalbard archipelago's most populous town. It is believed to be the most northerly permanent settlement in the entire world and is situated high in the Norwegian Arctic. The town, which has an airport, a school, a shopping mall, lodging options, dining establishments, and more, serves as the de facto "capital" of the islands.

Culture and History

The village, which was a significant mining location, is today becoming more and more well-known as a tourist destination. It is undoubtedly the best starting point for exploring Svalbard and is widely considered as the Arctic's most accessible frontier.

The Arctic Coal Company, which essentially founded the town in the early 1900s, was founded and presided over by American businessman John Munro Longyear, who is honored by the town's name.

The town is small enough to be easily navigated, and guests are always made to feel welcome. You might be astonished to find reindeers roaming freely in the town because it is a location where humans and environment coexist harmoniously in the delicate balance of life. Polar foxes could possibly be spotted if you're lucky.

Whether you want to be indoors or outdoors, whether you want to see or prefer to do, Longyearbyen has a lot to offer visitors.

Longyearbyen annually holds the popular Dark Season Blues Festival in late October. The "black season," when the sun and daylight are about to leave Svalbard and be absorbed by the lengthy, icy winter, begins with this event. Arctic Tapas are a treat for gourmands who enjoy the unexpected. Svalbard specialties like seal and whale are available in a few restaurants.

Svalbard Museum

Attractions & Activities

The Spitsbergen Airship Museum features artifacts and memorabilia from the age of polar exploration, which was largely accomplished by aircraft. The Svalbard Gallery features both ongoing and recurring exhibitions by Svalbard-based artists. The Svalbard Museum houses numerous exhibits regarding the archipelago's human history, particularly the whaling and mining industries, as well as a number of displays about polar flora and fauna.

The northernmost church in the world is located at Longyearbyen. It is constantly open and offers tourists coffee and pastries. Additionally, you can purchase books, postcards, and other little goods here. The 24-Hour Sundial is an amazing object that is close to the cathedral. Due to the constant sunshine over the endless summer days, it is obviously one of very few sundials in the world that can make this claim.

The numerous tour businesses in Svalbard provide a wide range of activities, such as hiking, dog sledding, kayaking, snowmobile safaris, and even coal mining. The Esmarkbreen Glacier, which is across the bay and reachable by boat in around 3 hours, has stunning blue hues that you shouldn't miss.

Bodo

A stunning coastline surrounds Bod, providing many options for exploring. Bodo is another lovely location from which to take in the mysterious dances of the Northern Lights as they flicker across the night sky. It is a gorgeous peninsula in Northern Norway. There are many more reasons to visit, albeit this is just the beginning.

Bodo has much to offer whether you find solace in the outdoors or prefer the urban thrills of a metropolis or town. A quick flight from Oslo will take just over an hour, and it will take you to a completely different world.

Culture and History

The town of Bodo was established in 1816, and as the local fisheries prospered, it expanded quickly in the years that followed. The town's survival was apparently guaranteed even after the herring went on thanks to the large schools of herring that arrived there in the middle to late 1800s.

The Germans attacked Bodo during the war, as they did many other towns, and in 1940 the town was completely destroyed in less than two hours. Fortunately, the majority of the occupants had already left, but the recovery was gradual and the memories were sad. Bodo nonetheless regained all of its previous splendor. Over 47,000 people now call it home, and the town is still expanding quickly.

Bodo's itinerary for today is jam-packed with events and activities. Whether you prefer a morning of isolation painting along the breakwater, or whether you appreciate listening to a violin concert taking place on a city rooftop.

Fans of football will appreciate watching a game at Aspmyra Stadium. A number of museums are also packed with fascinating information and artifacts; one of these is the Aviation Museum, which has a number of aircraft on display.

Norwegian Aviation Museum

Attractions & Activities

The Saltstraumen, or world's strongest maelstrom, is visible only 33 kilometers from Bodo. Visitors at high tide will be rendered speechless as they awe the power of nature. 400 million m3 of water, moving at high to 20 knots, surges across the 150 m wide, 3 km long strait every six hours. This phenomena can create powerful whirlpools up to 10 meters in diameter and 5 meters deep.

Bodo has a secret, though—surprisingly, it's one of the top locations worldwide for an exciting day of fishing. Cod, saithe, wolf fish, and halibut are just a few of the many types of fish that may be found in Saltstraumen. Here, a saithe fish weighing an astounding 22.7 kg became the record-holder for the saithe fish captured using a fishing pole. Visitors can participate in the sport by renting the necessary gear or going on an excursion with a pre-arranged group.

The world's densest population of white-tailed eagles, also known as sea eagles, is found in Bodo. These magnificent raptors are year-round residents of the region and can be seen flying through the air or perched on the rocks near the peninsula.

You can go kayaking in the middle of the night to embrace nature, or you can take a tour of the spectacular archipelago in a swift passenger boat. The adjacent islands are covered with a number of charming fishing towns, making a day trip spent exploring them and talking with the residents very intriguing.

Chapter 5: Famous Architectural Wonders in Norway

Norway is known for having incredibly diverse art and architectural styles. The architectural wonders of this nation serve as examples of typical Scandinavian architectural styles. If you visit the nation and take in its stunning architecture, you will undoubtedly be in awe. The elegant constructions of Norway are a fine representation of great taste and are well worth photographing and bringing back to your nation.

The National Museum Architecture, Oslo

The structure holds a special place in the history of Norwegian architecture. A quick glimpse at the building's architecture will leave you in awe. The structure is a fusion of many architectural styles. The structure, which was completed in 2008, had its primary portion created very early by Christian Heinrich Grosch. SverreFehn afterwards added to the building's architectural features. As was already said, the structure is a tasteful fusion of Classicist and Modernist styles, captivating travelers with its gorgeous design. If you are in Norway, you should definitely go there.

Utsikten Viewpoint, Gaularfjellet

Utsiken View Point, located in Gaularfjellet, is the spot for you if you enjoy outdoor pursuits like hiking and diving as well as views of Norway's picturesque wonders. The viewpoint is located in a picturesque area from which you can see the "country of waterfalls" in all its splendor. The viewpoint climbs to around 700 meters in height and is constructed on the cliff of a mountain. You may enjoy the calm weather there while taking in Norway's quiet environment, and the location will let you connect with the country's natural beauty.

Eggum, Lofoten

The location is actually a tourist rest area, but because to its illusionary design, it will appear more like an amphitheater, and you will be happy to realize that the rest area has been further molded to resemble an amphitheater. The location is perfect for viewing the Midnight Sun, and when visiting this area, you can really appreciate how beautiful nature is. Since there aren't many tourists at this location, you can have your correct peace of mind and spirit while you're there. The amphitheater-like construction of the rest area is a strong representation of antidilluvian buildings found around the world. Discover one of Norway's largest unspoiled natural wonders.

Karmoy Fishery Museum, Rogaland

Since 1950, fishing activities have been mechanized in Rogaland, and this museum will accurately depict the change in Norwegian fishing practices. The Fishery Museum's building is quite substantial and symbolizes the male elements connected to fishing. The museum has a distinctive style, and you can truly experience the nation's fishing industry there. The fishing museum also includes a number of aquariums that exhibit the many fish species found in Norway. Visit the area if you enjoy fishing and other aquatic activities to experience one of the most vibrant local cultures in the nation.

StokkoyaSjosenter, Stokkvika, Trondelag

When you visit this location, you will undoubtedly enjoy relaxing in Mother Nature's lap because of the unique design that brings people and the natural world into intimate contact. In order to create this location, the exclusive Norwegian Coastline and the Mediterranean Club were carefully blended. Once you've been here, you can experience a captivating connection with the beach's surroundings. You can unwind amidst the clear skies and verdant scenery while your children play nearby in the appropriate and secure areas that are present. It is definitely worth taking the time to appreciate the area's natural color palette.

Tverrfjellhytta, Dovre

Nearly 1.5 kilometers separate you from Tverrfjellhytta, where you can hike while admiring the breathtaking views of Norway. While the location provides great vantage points from which to view the area's many regions, if you want even better views, you'll need to hike higher. The location is along Main Road E6 in the Dovrefjell Mountains of Norway. You can always visit this location if you are traveling to Norway, but be sure to hike because else you will lose out on a key aspect of the location.

The Petter Das Museum, Alstahaug

A very well-known poet from Norway is named PetterDass. This poet led a very intriguing, bold, and passionate life. We can assure you that the museum will educate you about the regional literary traditions of Norway. The poet's courageous life is portrayed in the museum. The location is close to Sandnessjoen, which is a coastal town on the Helgeland Peninsula. The Alstahaug church from the Middle Ages and the Old Vicarage are two of Norway's most significant buildings, and the museum's designs have been created to give it an intriguing approach.

Trollveggen Visitor Center, More OgRomesdal

The tallest rock face on the entire European continent is located here. The main draw of this location is that it is almost 3,300 feet tall and completely vertical. The location's architecture is really strange, and it also has a variety of cafés and restaurants where you may have your refreshments while enjoying the location. The cafes offer travelers sweeping views of the area because they are facing the mountain wall. This is one of Norway's most popular tourist destinations. Once you've been here, you can enjoy the numerous aspects of nature.

You will undoubtedly be drawn to Norway City by such amazing architectural marvels. You must essentially see them because Norway's government continually indulges in various preservation techniques for its magnificent locations.

Best Beach Destinations in Norway

One of the world's top beaches is in Norway. You will undoubtedly get a sense of beauty as you approach the beaches in their magnificent manner. We advise you to check out the majority of the nation's beaches. While exploring the beaches, you can take advantage of the best sea points. The names and characteristics of the numerous beaches in Norway are shown here.

Ingiersstrand, Oslo

The beachfront property underwent renovation in 1934 from its original layout. When the beach was first depicted by SchistadMostue in the year 1934, it had the unfortunate circumstance of drawing a very vast diversity of crowds. The beach depicts one of Norway's top vacation and adventure spots. In essence, you have to go to the beach and hang out there. You will feel tethered to nature by the sparkling water and lovely sand. The greatest time to visit the beach is from May through September, which is considered the peak tourist season. On a weekly basis, from Friday to Sunday, a restaurant is open. After wandering about on the beach, you can enjoy your food and drinks in the restaurant.

Akrasanden, Karmoy

For a very long time, the Akrasanden in Karmoy held the title of most gorgeous beach in Norway. Even today, a large number of people frequent the beach mostly due to its attractiveness. You can enjoy a lovely view of the stunning surroundings as well as the beach's crystal-clear sea. The white sand on the beach is truly unique and will be adored by your children and family members. Once on the beach, you can feel the genuine Mediterranean ambiance, and the surroundings nearby offer many of options for hiking and other activities. Always make use of them.

Ramberg, Lofoten

The Lofoten beach known as Ramberg is occasionally referred to as the "pearl of Lofoten." The beach is an unquestionable asset for tourists coming to Norway. The Lofoten Beach is located not far from the road, and getting there from the road is fairly simple. The RambergGjestegard, located on the Ramberg Beach in Lofoten, will serve you incredibly tasty Norwegian cuisine. You are welcome to eat lunch there. The Adventure Company of Lofoten provides you with a range of creative ways to spend time on the beach. You can attempt surfing, paddle boarding, and snorkeling.

Bystranda, Kristiansand

The beach area is really fascinating and has diverse elements like palm trees, etc. There are very few beaches in the world, not just in Norway, that can compare to the magnificence of this beach. The beach's natural beauty is highly representative of beaches around the world. It feels serene and quiet because of the surrounding palm trees. Given that it is located in the center of Kristiansand, the place's position is what gives it its name. The beach is mostly a terrific summer location; if you visit during the summer, you can expect to have exceptionally pleasant weather.

Mjelle, Bodo

The coastline is a short distance from Bodo. For transportation to the location, a car is available. The beach location is remote from the city's center and is serene and quiet. The beach is the ideal location for you if you intend to spend your time alone. You can appreciate the sound of the waves while taking a solitary stroll along the expansive length of sand. TerjeNilson was the first to create a song about this location, which ultimately gave it international fame. While strolling around the Mjelle beach, take pleasure in the genuine Norwegian way of life.

Hauklandstranda, Lofoten

Huakland Beach is situated in a spectacular area of the middle of Lofoten. The beach's primary site can be reached by a large number of vehicles due to its centralized location, which makes it quite simple to get to. The beach is located on the northern side of the Vestvagoy and is about ten minutes' drive from Leknes. In addition to taking in the beach's captivating landscape, you can also take use of the other amenities it offers, such as parking. Tourists have access to parking spaces right next to the beach, so you can quickly park your car there before going into the water.

Solastraden, Stravenger

Windsurfing enthusiasts should visit Solastraden in Stravenger, which is the right destination for you. When you stay at this beach, you can engage in a huge variety of activities. On the beach, there are organized activities like windsurfing and golf, among others. The golf course at the seaside is where visitors go to relax and have fun. You might mingle with the visitors to the golf course to engage in beneficial conversation. You can take advantage of the different spa services that the beach has to offer. Once you arrive at Stravenger's Solastraden Beach, there won't be a lack of things to do.

Orresanden, Jaeren

The longest beach in Norway is called Orresanden, and it can be found in the town of Jeren. The beach is constantly crowded with people throughout the year as visitors from all over the world go to view the nation's longest beach. You can engage in a variety of activities, including surfing. One of the most popular tourist locations in Norway is the beach, and almost all guidebooks and other travel materials will recommend visiting there. Take a mental break by taking a leisurely stroll down the beach. In Norway, the beach is a popular tourism location, therefore people frequently go there.

Chapter 6:
Best restaurants in Norway

The world's best cuisines may come from the Nordic region. The Norwegian people are very aware of their culture and traditions, which is also very important for portraying the nation's cuisine culture. If you are visiting Norway, we advise you to take advantage of the greatest dining options available. The top restaurants in Oslo are well-known worldwide and have garnered numerous accolades. You might stay in Norway for a longer period of time and only eat their delectable treats. We have included a list of all of our recommendations to assist you further on your vacation to Norway.

Maaemo.

Due to its delicious cuisine, it tops Norway's list of restaurants. If you don't eat at this restaurant while you're in Norway, you will undoubtedly be missing out on a significant portion of Norwegian cuisine. The restaurant's main appeal is its experimental approach to each and every dish, but you will also be given the best Norwegian meals with a beautiful touch of modernism. The establishment was awarded three Michelin stars in 2016, which contributed significantly to its elevation to one of the top spots in Norway. This restaurant uses a wide variety of flavors, which is also very important to how well it serves its customers. Be cautious of it.

Brewpub Aegir

The Aegir restaurant is close to the Flamsbana train station and offers its customers some of the best national specialties. Their varied beer experiments serve as their x-factor. The Aegir Brewpub has had success pairing different foods with beer and serving them to their customers. The restaurant is a stunning Viking hall that offers the best Viking menus in the area, which also happens to be the best tourist attractions. The restaurant uses entirely local ingredients to prepare its dishes, thus enhancing the best aspects of Nordic cuisine. Once at Aegir Brewpub, eat what the locals eat and take in the best of Norway.

Enhjorningen

The restaurant is located in Bryggen in Bergen, one of Norway's nicest and most picturesque neighborhoods. The main benefit of this restaurant is that it offers its patrons the best in scenic beauty in addition to delicious food. Enhhjorningen has a long history that dates back to the 13th century, and it has finally modernized to offer its visitors the best cuisine. The cuisine at this restaurant showcases the best aspects of Bergen culture. If you eat at this restaurant, you can indulge in the finest seafood and fish meals.

Mother India

One of Norway's top Indian restaurants is called Mother India. This accolade-winning eatery has been enjoying 22 years of prosperity while wallowing in glory. This restaurant, which is run by the well-known chef Sarita, is renowned for its incredible, delicious food. The atmosphere in the restaurant is extremely comfortable, and the staff members are really hospitable. You can choose from a number of fusion recipes that combine Norwegian and Indian flavors. The food can be a little hot for an Indian restaurant, but it's still worth tasting. You will want to order more once you've tried the food. The finest place to eat with your family and spend quality time with them is at this restaurant.

Mathus Peder Hiort

A small village in Norway by the name of Roros has several wooden buildings that appear like they belong on a postcard. You should try the local cuisine at Peder Hiort Mathus, which is a great restaurant in this area. Tourists also find the pizza menu to be appealing. The restaurant is constructed of wood and resembles a stunning work of wood art. The flower- and art-decorated interiors will be to your taste. It is a pleasure to eat here in this elegant restaurant. Although there are many various types of dishes available here, be sure to check out the specials. You may find a ton of combos here, from lunch to dinner.

Hoven Restaurant

Hoven Restaurant is the place to go if you want to eat somewhere affordable while also getting the best Norwegian food possible. The welcoming atmosphere at this eatery is well-known. This sleek restaurant offers a wide range of amenities and delicious food. This restaurant, which is perched on a cliff's edge, is ideal for its dramatic setting and offers some of the best views of Norway. In addition to this wonderful feature, this restaurant offers some of the most flavorful regional ingredients that go well with the surroundings. There are many different cuisines and excellent foods on the menu.

Gapahuken Restaurant

This restaurant, which is close to Kirkenes, is well-known for its setting because it offers the best panoramic views of Russia, which is only a short distance away. This restaurant's timber and glass construction gives it a chilly, calming, and comforting Norwegian vibe. You will get enough value from the chill in this restaurant's stunning and contemporary setting. In addition, Gapahuken is well known for its unique regional cuisine. The main feature of this restaurant is how the seasonal menu and local specialties fluctuate, allowing you to have a beautiful meal that will keep you healthy throughout the year. While visiting, sample the tastiest foods, including the wonderful local arctic salmon and reindeer as well as cloudberries.

Aunegarden

Aunegarden is a very old restaurant that has been there for at least 200 years. This restaurant is a superb example of a historical testimony to Norwegian history. This restaurant's current owner is well aware of it and takes extra precautions to protect it. This restaurant offers a wonderful old historical environment and has a colorful historical past. Once you're inside, you'll understand what it's like to feel "aged" and what it's like to spend hours there. Both an excellent selection of regional meals and other international cuisines are offered on the menu. The cooks constantly aim to serve something new to their customers and are quite inventive. The food at this restaurant is seasonal. Due to the utilization of organic and locally sourced ingredients, all of the dishes are delicious. When in Norway, you must eat at this restaurant.

Kulturhuset

This restaurant has recently expanded, taking up the full fourth floor and backyard of the building from which it previously operated. Different courses will be offered on each floor. For example, the ground floor is designated for breakfast, where you can order the breakfast item and coffee of your choice. This place is renowned for its amazing food and atmosphere that is similar to a hangout spot for friends. Along with a fantastic selection of cheese, this place has a good wine selection. The beer bar is on the second floor, where all the fun is. Enjoy the large book selection in the library as well. Literally, you could spend the entire day here working, reading, and enjoying some of the fantastic food that is served. Additionally, there is a game area where you may have fun while enjoying a delicious beer.

Vippa

In Norway, do you want to have a great time? Vippa will be the ideal location for you, especially if you are a foodie and are constantly looking for different types of cuisine. The newest pub in the city where you can enjoy some of the best Norwegian cuisine and some of the best music is this restaurant, which is situated on the outskirts of the Oslo Port. You can order everything from Vietnamese cuisine to Chinese delicacies and Syrian Shawarma. The greatest times to visit this restaurant are on Sunday and Thursday, when it plays the loudest music and has some of the top DJs. From fine wines to craft brews, Vippa has all the best beverages. One of the nicest views you will ever see in Norway is the sunset over the Oslo fjord, so be sure not to miss it.

Chapter 7:
The Best Accommodation In Norway

Norway takes its cue from nature when it comes to its most distinctive lodgings, whether it's a swanky design-driven hotel at the foot of extraordinarily tall mountains, a cutting-edge urban retreat hugging the shores of a deeper-than-blue fjord, or a log cabin filled with rustic, fire-warmed romance tucked away in forests where reindeer roam. If you're looking for an ultra-luxe boutique hideaway with a Michelin-starred restaurant in the basement or an igloo that has just been freshly molded with the first significant snowfall of the winter, Norway can be explored in entirely new and exciting ways when you venture beyond the avalanche of cookie-cutter chains.

The Norwegians are experts at metamorphosis; they take pleasure in giving outdated constructions a fresh start. Think of the dilapidated barns, banks, and trading posts from the 16th century that have been converted into opulent hotels with distinctive personalities and the work of renowned architects. Even though the hotels are expensive, it's worth it to see the aurora as it swings above the high Arctic mountains covered in snow and ice and to see the rising sun illuminate the intricate network of fjords.

1. Isbreen The Glacier, Troms og Finnmark

The black Finnmark Alps rise majestically above the steel-blue Jkelfjord in this beautiful spot, where a glacier empties directly into the water, far north of the Arctic Circle. The modern glass igloos or geodesic domes are coolly understated in true Scandi style if the surroundings are dramatic: icy palettes of blues and grays, goose-down comforters, sleekly designed furniture, wood-fired stoves, telescopes, and expansive windows for viewing the fjord, stars, and northern lights. Upon returning from a day of whale watching, dog sledding, ski touring, or rowing out to the glacier, your hosts prepare feasts of local reindeer, fish, and berries. Oh, and did we forget to mention the sauna and the outdoor hot tub near the water? Isbreen is always reachable, but in the winter it is entirely Narnia.

2. Odda, Woodnest, and Vestland

When Kjartan wanted to propose to the Sydney native who is the love of his life, he built Sally the treehouse of her wildest dreams instead of dropping down on one knee and opening a ring box. This established the groundwork for the surprising withdrawal. These environmentally friendly, wood, shingle-covered tree houses in Odda are poised like eyries in towering pines above the Hardanger Fjord, which is ringed by mountains and is sapphire blue. They were designed to mimic Norwegian pinecones. They can only be reached by a challenging upward hike. With the aid of architects, black alder interiors with handcrafted furniture, underfloor heating, and wraparound windows framing fjord views were created. Breakfast consists of locally produced sourdough, eggs, juice, and coffee.

3. The Storfjord Hotel in Romsdal.

Storfjord is a collection of dark-timbered, turf-roofed buildings on a hillside with views of the Sunnmore Alps and Storfjord's west coast. It couldn't be more Norwegian. Candles, fireplaces, a private spa with a jacuzzi that views out over a forest, and a low-key gourmet menu that emphasizes local ingredients are some of the attractions at the boutique resort. The nouveau-rustic rooms include carved log walls, subdued hues, tweeds, and down comforters, giving them a comfortable, hug-like atmosphere. Borrow boats, snowshoes, walking sticks, and fishing equipment (these seas have some big cod that can be caught). Or look for a peaceful place where you can write, read, rest, and dream.

4. Alta Sorrisniva

The aurora regularly dances in the clear night sky of Alta, located in the high Arctic, as you might anticipate from the town that is home to the Northern Lights Cathedral. Snow-covered Sorrisniva looks gorgeous in the winter. After a day of snowshoeing, tobogganing, dog or reindeer sledding, you may spend a surprisingly delightful night on an ice bed wrapped in reindeer hide. Its igloos are constructed by ice sculptors. Even better, you may take a two-hour crash course in ice sculpture for the chance to express your creativity. For dinners expertly prepared with locally obtained reindeer, moose, seafood, and wild berries, drinks at the ice bar warm you up nicely. If you wish to get married, there is even a church made of ice.

5. Hotel Eilert Smith in Stavanger

With only 12 specially built rooms that match the building's 1930s architecture and a two-Michelin-starred, 25-seat RE-NAA restaurant in the basement, Eilert Smith in Stavanger, a city on a fjord, fully nails the phrase "boutique." This hotel was designed by architects who were interested in the avant-garde while scrupulously conserving the original curves, geometric patterns, and modernist materials like travertine, brass, marble, and wood. There is made-to-order furniture, pure colors, and a special light that comes in through the little horizontal windows. Plump for the rooftop residence with its views of the Stavanger port and spiral staircase encircling it.

6. Basecamp Explorer, Spitsbergen's Longyearbyen

Polar bears outnumber humans on the archipelago of Svalbard, the last untouched part of Norway before the North Pole. Longyearbyen, located on the island of Spitsbergen, is the world's most northerly settlement and the final hub of modernity. During the winter, riding a dog sled or snowmobile while the aurora bursts across the sky is the greatest way to enjoy this magical place. It is a region of icy beauty and bone-chilling cold. Conservation-focused The magnificent base Basecamp Explorer is designed to resemble a modern-rustic trapper's lodge. In addition to a comfortable lounge where you may unwind after an expedition, it has rooms decorated with driftwood, maps, and pictures of explorers. Even better, they arrange a variety of fun events including multi-day snowmobile expeditions into the Arctic proper, dog sledding, and glacier tours.

7. **Angvik Gamle Handelssted**

West Norwegian's Tingvoll Fjord's northern bank is home to this lovely white-washed, timber-fronted hotel. Ships from Holland went here to acquire timber in the 1500s, making it a mouthwatering illustration of legacy that has been conserved. Classic design motifs like calming grays and creams, cozy lighting, and dressed-up antiques are present in the majority of the rooms. They also have calmingly beautiful fjord views. The restaurant is a more traditional, rustic setting, and the chef enjoys utilizing local farms and fjords for his menu. The deciding factor, though, is Badehuset Spa, which provides opulent treatments, hot baths, and a sauna and is housed in a restored, glass-walled 18th-century granary overlooking the fjord.

8. Hotel Brosundet, Alesund

On a peninsula jutting into the North Sea is Alesund, one of Norway's busiest and most appealing port cities. Mirror copies of a row of gabled, candy-colored art nouveau houses were created in the Brosundet canal. This modest, family-run firm combines distinctive architecture with a minimalist edge and contemporary beauty in its rebuilt fishing warehouse. The foyer, which rises to a central gallery, is ablaze. With exposed beams and arched windows that reference the Nordic design, the rooms are painted in shades of white, chocolate, and charcoal. A cocktail bar, a glam exercise and spa area, and the highly respected restaurant Apotekergata No. 5 are just a few of the features they have taken into account. The ideal accommodation for romance is Room 47 in the Molja Lighthouse at the end of the jetty.

9. Opus 16 in Bergen

The family of Edvard Grieg runs this upscale, classic hotel as a monument to the 19th-century Norwegian pianist and composer. The building, which was formerly Bergen's poshest bank, harkens back to its historic past with marble columns, polished granite, and substantial chandeliers while making a clear transition into more modern territory with streamlined furnishings, unique wall coverings, and irregular bursts of brilliant color. You are in the midst of everything on Vgsallmenningen, one of Bergen's most gorgeous squares. You are only a few feet away from the fish market, the famed Bryggen shoreline, and the funicular that ascends Mount Floyen. The stylish brasserie offers afternoon tea with a touch of sophistication and hosts live jazz performances on Sundays.

10. Solvorn's Walaker Hotel on Sognefjord

Walaker is situated in a surreal setting on the shores of Lustrafjord, which reaches out in an amazingly blue finger to touch the steep, glaciated slopes of Jotunheimen and Jostedalsbreen national parks. This is where you'll find Norway's oldest hotel. The Nitter family has owned and run this historic inn since 1690, and it could care less about the present. The cream-timber villa is situated in lush floral gardens that descend to the fjord and has heavy antique furnishings and wall coverings in each of its rooms. Dinner is provided at precisely 7.30 p.m. and includes fjord-fished seafood, woodland venison, mushrooms, and fruits. You'll remember and fawn about the Walaker Hotel for the rest of your life since it's retro and idyllically perfect.

Chapter 8: Best Souvenirs to buy in Norway.

Chocolates

One of the best European treats is actually the numerous chocolates. Once you are in Norway, you can always use them. You may purchase these chocolates and the nicest chocolates in almost any store in the nation. Once you are in Norway, you can purchase a wide range of different goods, including straightforward and simple chocolate bars and a variety of candy. The chocolate bars' flavors are quite inventive, and they come in almost every flavor imaginable. You can choose from a wide variety of bars and candies in the lavishly designed candy shops in Norway. You can perform the necessary study on Norway's top confectionery shops and take advantage of them. Among the many sweets sold in Norway, salty liquor ice is a highly well-liked treat. It consistently maintains the top spot among the other sweets thanks to its distinctive flavor. The sweet flavor of the candy will gradually start to taste more like the salty liquor ice found in Norway, which will further pique the curiosity of candy enthusiasts. Even though many candy companies around the world have begun to copy the phenomena of salty liquor ice, the unique Norway sweet is always a one-of-a-kind, therefore you must essentially have it.

Sweets from Norway

The finest memento to bring home from Norway is likely to be a sweet treat. Norway offers a huge selection of sweets to its visitors, and many people are eager to sample the best of Norway. When visiting Norway, you should try some of the local treats. Many individuals taste them and bring them back to their homes for their friends and family. Many stores display a broad selection of sweets in their shop windows; you may choose from them and enjoy the best flavors of Norway, albeit you must first conduct some study on the best sweets before traveling there. When you arrive in the country, take advantage of the wide selection of pancakes and other delicious bakery delicacies that are waiting for you. You can find a cake that is well encircled by strawberry treats and is the classic variation in every street and byway of the nation. You can find a bakery and order your favorite sweet dish, or choose from a variety of other cakes that are filled with delicacies. You will definitely be impressed by the sweets' amazing patterns.

Vikings

Another cultural tradition that is well-known in Norway is that of the Vikings. The Vikings initially lived in Scandinavia's coastal regions, from which they traveled to the nation of Norway. The ferocity, cruelty, and bravery of the Vikings can be used by the Norwegian people to illustrate the distinct Viking civilizations. The Vikings have a strong historical presence in Norway's culture. Today, a number of Norwegian trinkets connected to the Vikings have become very well known. The Viking pendants, fortunate charms, and other trinkets have drawn all kinds of travelers to Norway. Norway has been successful in paying significant homage to the native Viking culture. If you enjoy gathering such legendary or historical mementos, consider gathering a Vikings memento and bringing it home. You will undoubtedly be enthralled by the race's cultural magnificence.

Lucky Trolls

Trolls were said to have been the first people to live in Norway, and according to local folklore, they still do. The best time to expect to see trolls emerge from their hiding places is at dusk. When you are on a lonesome walk through a forest and you notice a flicker of light, you might run across a troll there. A troll is staring at you if you notice a flash of light in the deserted woodland. In Norway, trolls are a significant aspect of the country's culture. You can learn more about the trolls' cultural aspects. Numerous trolls are seen as lucky in Norway, and as a result, the lucky trolls are frequently sold in the nation's shops. The lucky trolls you bring home will be treasured by you and your loved ones as a fascinating souvenir. Keep an eye out for the mementos and essentially purchase them. It is typically advised to adhere to the local culture when visiting a location outside of your familiar surroundings. The lucky numbers will also help to keep the people you care about safe.

The Decorations in Pewter

The Norwegian people have amazing craftsmanship and other things. They were inspired to produce the best handicrafts throughout the Roman era in Norway, and this tradition is still alive today. A beautiful present or keepsake from Norway is pewter. You can give the present to a friend or a member of your family. In Norway, pewter is used to symbolize special occasions like weddings and homecomings. The joyous Norwegian holidays are closely linked to pewter. Pewter can be combined with different types of tin and copper to create a new chemical compound that elevates the object's level of splendor. Norway has a huge market for pewter ornaments, and you may find the best of them at Norwegian stores. Look for the best, and we are confident that you won't want to skimp when buying gifts for your loved ones. These exquisite pewters include many motifs that pay homage to Norway's historic culture. If you get the proper item, the rich cultures will certainly accompany you home. Even if Norway won't provide you any bogus goods, make sure you bring the appropriate things home.

Conclusion

Norway is one of the most well-liked tourist destinations in the world, and for good reason. Even though visiting the Norwegian fjords is very simple, there are still a few travel tips for Norway that you should be aware of to make the most of your trip, especially if it is your first time there.

In our what to know before visiting Norway guide, you'll find details on the Top Attractions, Best Accommodations, Food and Drinks, Norway Visa Requirements, the Cost of Travel to Norway, and much more.

This comprehensive travel guide would provide you with all the knowledge you need if you were thinking about visiting Norway this year, which you should do without a doubt.

Made in the USA
Monee, IL
18 June 2023